Questions You Never Thought You'd Ask

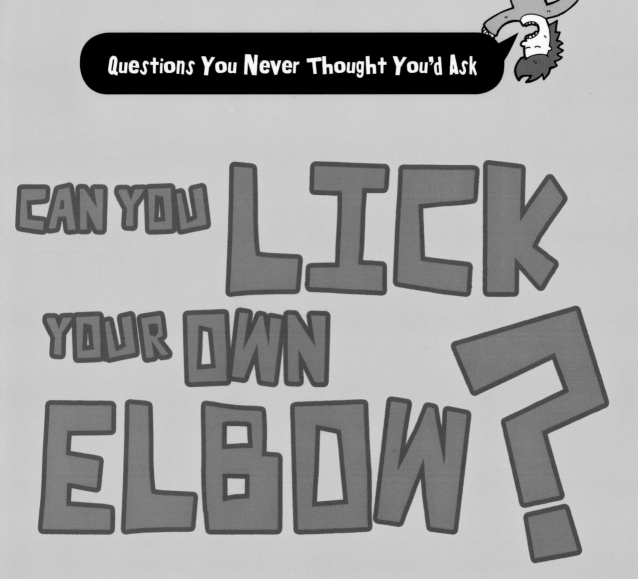

CAN YOU LICK YOUR OWN ELBOW?

And Other Questions About The Human Body

Paul Mason

Raintree

Chicago, Illinois

Edited by Dan Nunn, Rebecca Rissman,
  and John-Paul Wilkins
Designed by Steve Mead
Picture research by Mica Brancic
Production by Sophia Argyris
Originated by Capstone Global Library Ltd
Printed and bound in China by CTPS

17 16 15 14 13
10 9 8 7 6 5 4 3 2 1

Library of Congress Cataloging-in-Publication Data
Cataloging-in-Publication data is available at the
Library of Congress: loc.gov

ISBN 978-1-4109-5201-1 (hardback)
ISBN 978-1-4109-5207-3 (paperback)

Acknowledgments
We would like to thank the following for permission
to reproduce photographs: © Capstone p. 10 boy
(Karon Dubke); Getty Images p. 20 man sneezing
(Blend Images/John Lund); Photoshot p. 25 (World
Illustrated/© De Agostini), Sam dei lune p. 5;
Shutterstock pp. 4 (© photobank.ch), 6 brain (© Jeff
Banke), 6 hammer (© Ljupco Smokovski), 7 (© VILevi),
8 (© Yuri Arcurs), 9 ears (© Aidar), 9 elderly man (©
Valentina R.), 10 girl in field (© Eduard Stelmakh), 11 (©
Kacso Sandor), 12 baby (© aporokh at gmail dot com),
12 monster truck (© Gunter Nezhoda), 13 (© mast3r),
14, 15 baby (© Photocrea), 14, 15 horse (© smereka),
16 (© Kacso Sandor), 17 (© Ariwasabi), 18 (© Martin
Novak), 19 duster (© Africa Studio), 19 gorilla (© Elliot
Hurwitt), 20 cheetah (© photobar), 21 (© Shebeko), 22
criying man (© doglikehorse), 22 bed (© Viktor1), 22
roast duck (© Maksim Toome), 23 top left pig (© Eric
Isselée), 23 top right pig, bottom left pig, bottom right
pig (© Tsekhmister), 23 wings (© Wallenrock), 23 man
(© ARENA Creative), 24 tree (© majeczka), 24 man's
tongue (© photobank.ch), 26 (© Africa Studio), 27
(© Reha Mark), 28 man with magnifying glass
(© BonD80), 28 man with tongue out (© Dedyukhin
Dmitry), 29 (© Cupertino).

Cover photographs of funny man (© photobank.ch)
and bicep muscle of thin woman (© Steven Frame)
reproduced with permission of Shutterstock.

We would like to thank Diana Bentley and Marla Conn
for their invaluable help in the preparation of this book.

Every effort has been made to contact copyright
holders of any material reproduced in this book. Any
omissions will be rectified in subsequent printings if
notice is given to the publisher.

CONTENTS

Some words are shown in bold, **like this**. You can find out what they mean by looking in the glossary.

CAN YOU LICK YOUR OWN ELBOW?

Ninety-nine percent of people try to lick their elbow after reading that question! If you did, too, you probably decided it is impossible.

In fact, a few very **flexible** people *can* manage to get their tongue barely touching their elbow.

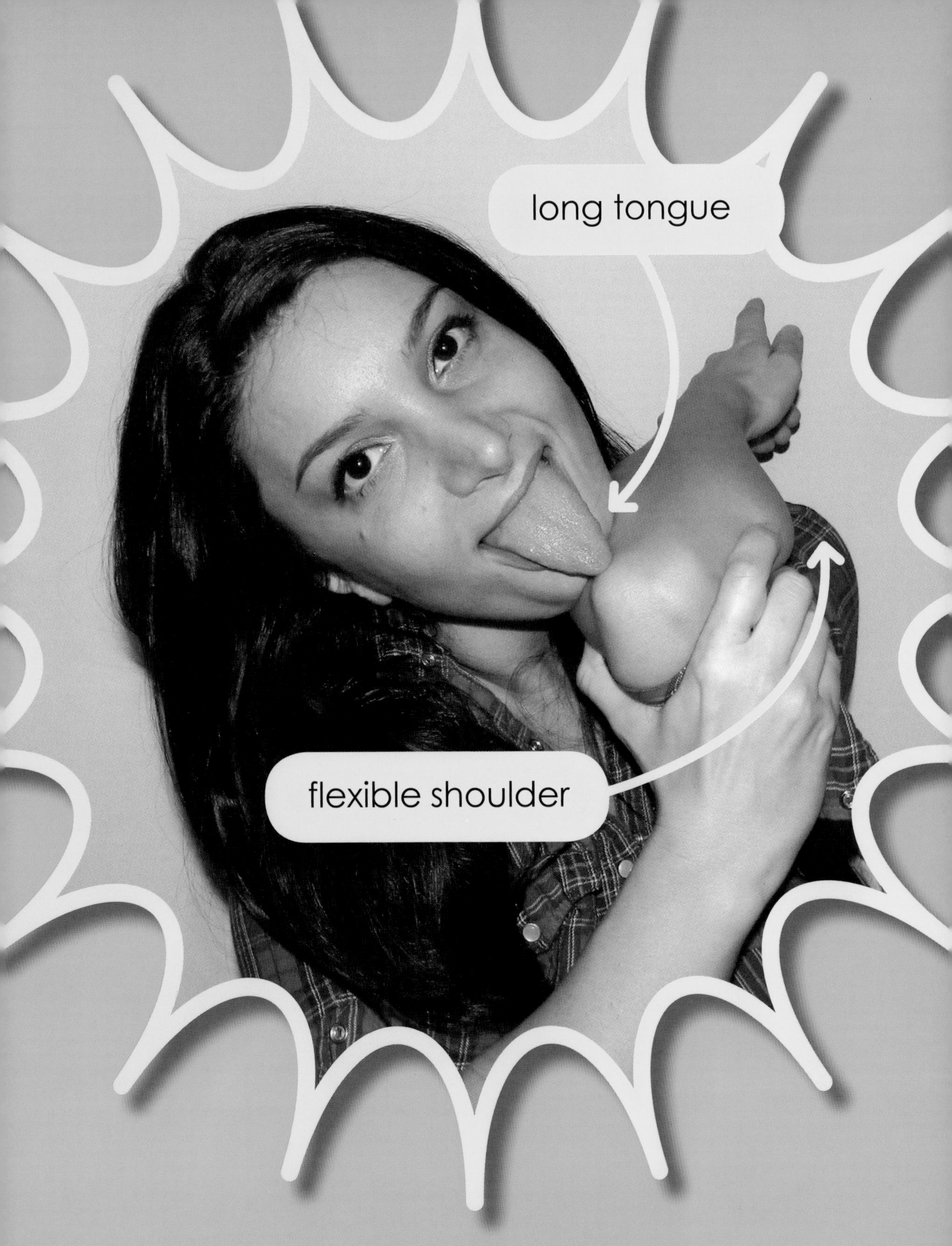
long tongue
flexible shoulder

CAN YOUR BRAIN FEEL PAIN?

No! Your brain can tell when *another* part of you is feeling pain. But your brain itself has no pain **sensors** in it. That is why your brain cannot feel any pain.

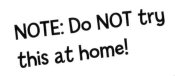

NOTE: Do NOT try this at home!

Did you know?
Because the brain does not feel pain, people sometimes have **brain surgery** while they are still awake.

WILL **I** KEEP GROWING FOREVER?

No, you will not keep growing forever. Most people stop growing taller when they are about 16 or 17 years old. Then, after the age of about 40, people start to shrink!

spine shortens

bones may get smaller

By the age of 80, most people are 1 to 3 inches shorter.

Did you know?
Your ears and your nose never stop growing. But after you are born, your eyes hardly grow at all.

DO GIRLS SMELL BETTER THAN BOYS?

When it comes to **sweat**, yes! During and after **puberty**, female sweat is quite a lot less stinky than male sweat. Girls also sweat less than boys.

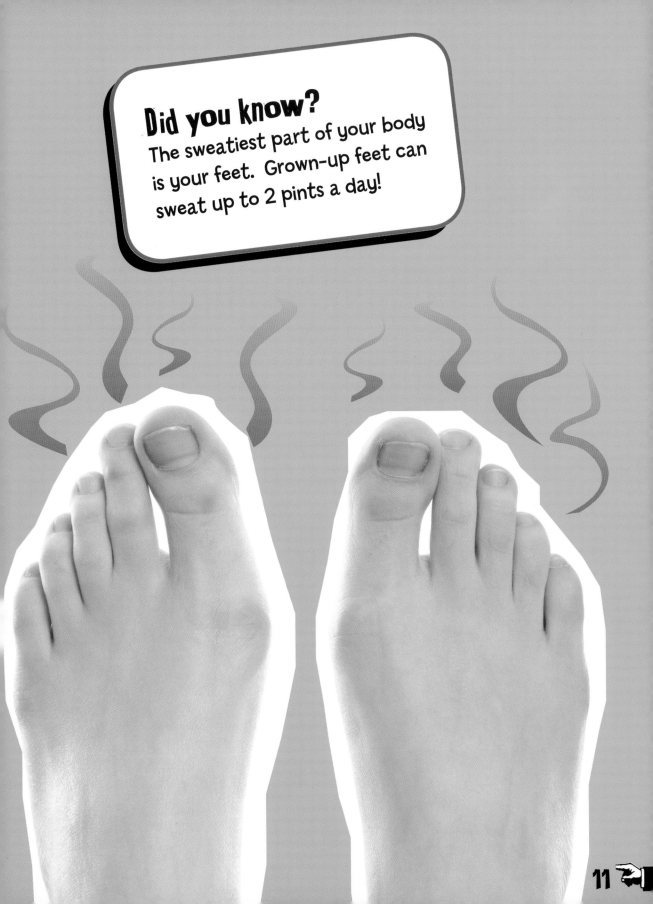

COULD YOU PICK UP A CAR?

You could not pick up a whole car and hold it over your head. But humans *have* lifted cars using only their muscles. It usually happens when someone is very scared. Fear causes your body to release a substance called **adrenaline**. This supercharges your muscles.

eyes send message: DANGER!
brain approves release of adrenaline
muscles become supercharged

WHICH IS STRONGER— A BABY OR A WORK HORSE?

A horse that weighs nearly 1 ton is *much* stronger than a 9-pound baby, obviously. That is why babies are not good at pulling carts and carrying heavy loads!

OK...

However, babies have more strength per pound of weight than work horses. That means a baby weighing almost a ton would be stronger than a work horse!

Get out of the way!

15

ARE THERE PEOPLE WHO DON'T FART?

No—everyone farts, even teachers! It is just that some people are better at hiding it than others. Farting is caused by swallowing air and by **digestion**. The only way not to fart would be not to breathe or eat!

food and air in

digestion

exhaust
gas out

Did you know?
People fart an average of 14 times a day.

CAN YOU TICKLE YOURSELF?

No! Feeling ticklish is caused by a fear of being touched by someone else. That is why we wriggle and try to get away. If we try to tickle ourselves, our brain knows not to be scared. That is why we do not react in the same way.

Did you know?
Some animals, including apes and rats, are ticklish, just like humans.

Imagine being asked to find out whether gorillas like being tickled!

IS YOUR SNEEZE FASTER THAN A CHEETAH?

Cheetahs are the fastest land animals. They have been recorded running at 75 miles per hour. But some people say that sneezes travel even faster, at 100 miles per hour!

In fact, this is not true. Sneezes only travel at about 40 miles per hour.

Did you know?
No matter how much you try, it is impossible to sneeze with your eyes open.

WHICH CAN YOU GO LONGER WITHOUT— FOOD OR SLEEP?

You feel hungry every few hours, but sleepy only at nighttime. So, it must be sleep, right? Wrong! A healthy human can last weeks without food. (Do NOT try it, though—it is very bad for you!)

The longest anyone has ever managed without sleep is 11 days. By the end, he was having **hallucinations**!

COULD YOU UPROOT TREES WITH YOUR TONGUE?

No—but it is not as silly a question as it sounds. Your tongue is made of muscles, like an elephant's trunk. And elephants *do* uproot trees with their trunks. With a big enough tongue, maybe you could do the same!

Did you know?
A human tongue once lifted almost 26 pounds. That is the same as two human babies. Ouch!

WHO HAS MORE BONES— A BABY OR A GROWN-UP?

You might think it would be a big grown-up—but you would be wrong! Babies have 50 percent more bones. As you get older, some of your bones **fuse** together. So, you start life with about 300, but end up with just over 200.

full of bones

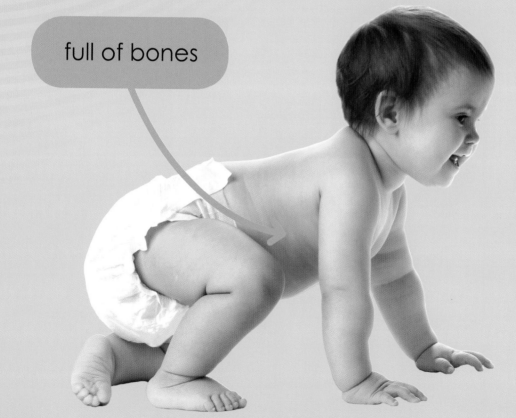

only two-thirds
as many bones
as a baby

Did you know?
About a quarter of your
bones are in your feet.

WHY DO CROOKS WEAR GLOVES?

Crooks wear gloves so that they do not leave fingerprints behind. There are other prints crooks could leave behind, though. For example, everyone has a **unique** tongue. Imagine catching a criminal using only his tongue print!

Just stick out your tongue please, sir. Aha!

Did you know?

Everyone's ear is slightly different, so ear prints have been used to identify criminals.

GLOSSARY

adrenaline substance released by the body during frightening or exciting situations. It causes the heart to beat faster and allows the muscles to work better.

brain surgery operation in which the brain itself is cut open

digestion breaking down food into useful parts and waste as it passes through your body

flexible capable of bending and being able to move joints—such as the elbows, back, or neck—farther than most people

fuse join together

hallucination vision of something that is not actually there, which often seems scary or confusing

puberty time when a child's body starts to become adult, or grown-up

sensor something able to detect a physical sensation, such as heat, light, or pain

sweat moisture that comes out through your skin when you are hot. Sweating helps to cool your body down.

unique one of a kind

FIND OUT MORE

Books

Bailey, Gerry, and Steve Way. *Body and Health: Discover Science Through Facts and Fun (Simply Science)*. Pleasantville, N.Y.: Gareth Stevens, 2009.

Ballard, Carol, and Steve Parker. Body Focus series. Chicago: Heinemann Library, 2009.

Parker, Steve. *The Human Body Book*. New York: Dorling Kindersley, 2007.

Rake, Jody Sullivan. *Why Feet Smell and Other Gross Facts About Your Body (First Facts)*. Mankato, Minn.: Capstone, 2012.

Web sites

Facthound offers a safe, fun way to find Internet sites related to this book. All of the sites on Facthound have been researched by our staff.

Here's all you do:
Visit www.facthound.com
Type in this code: 9781410952011

INDEX